GO FACTS NATURAL DISASTERS
Volcano

Volcano

contents

© Blake Publishing 2006
Additional material © A & C Black Publishers Ltd 2006

First published in Australia in 2006 by Blake Education Pty Ltd

This edition published in the United Kingdom in 2006 by
A & C Black Publishers Ltd, 38 Soho Square, London W1D 3HB
www.acblack.com

Hardback edition
ISBN-10: 0-7136-7956-5
ISBN-13: 978-0-7136-7956-4

Paperback edition
ISBN-10: 0-7136-7964-6
ISBN-13: 978-0-7136-7964-9

A CIP record for this book is available from the British Library.

Written by Ian Rohr
Publisher: Katy Pike
Editor: Paul O'Beirne
Design and layout by The Modern Art Production Group

Photo credits: p5 (br) picture courtesy NASA; Title page, p5 (tr), p6 (tl),
p11 (top), p16 (br), p19 (tl, tr), p21 (tl), p25 (tl, br), p27 (tl, tr, bl),
p28 (tl, centre), p29 (australian picture library); p19 (bl) (photolibrary); pp12–13
(Paul McEvoy); Illustrations on pp4, 7 and 9: Toby Quarmby.

Printed in China by WKT Company Ltd.

What is a Volcano?

The solid ground that we walk on is part of the Earth's crust. Below this crust lies an intensely hot layer of molten rock, known as magma. When magma explodes through an opening in the Earth's crust, a volcano erupts.

Volcanoes can be cone-shaped mountains or they can be wide, sloping hills. They can also appear under the sea. When a break in the Earth's surface allows molten rock to come up from the Earth's core, a volcano is formed. When molten rock hits the surface it is called lava.

time after an eruption, the land lies ruined and deserted. One of nature's most frightening and fantastic events, volcanoes have a massive impact on landscape. They bury towns and create islands and mountains. Volcanoes truly change the world.

Volcanoes and us

Throughout history, major volcanic eruptions have killed large numbers of people. Volcanoes can trigger mud slides, floods and **tsunamis**, and fast moving waves of boiling, poisonous gases. For a long

Active, dormant or extinct

Volcanoes that have erupted recently, or are likely to soon, are called active. Dormant volcanoes haven't erupted for a long time but still could. Extinct volcanoes are no longer volcanic.

Active   Dormant   Extinct

Lava erupts at temperatures of up to 1200 °C.

Volcanoes can generate fantastic lightning storms. The storms are caused by the friction between rapidly twirling particles of rock and ash.

There are 500 active volcanoes around the world. Approximately 60 erupt every year.

GO FACT!

DID YOU KNOW?

There are volcanoes on other planets. The gigantic Olympus Mons on Mars is 25 kilometres high and 600 kilometres wide.

5

How Volcanoes are Formed

Volcanoes form when hot magma pushes its way through Earth's crust. Earth's crust is made up of separate pieces, known as tectonic plates. These plates fit together like a giant jigsaw puzzle. Volcanoes form when these plates interact.

Colliding plates

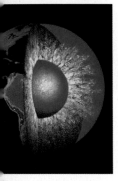

There are seven large tectonic plates and many smaller ones, all of them moving. Underneath Earth's crust is the **mantle**. The outer layer is hard, but the inner layer is partly melted. The tectonic plates move on this soft layer.

Subduction volcanoes

Often when plates collide, the heavier plate slides underneath the lighter plate. This is called subduction. As the lower plate is pushed down into the hot mantle, it melts and becomes magma.

This new magma mixes with trapped steam and gases in the **magma chamber**. Pressure from surrounding rocks forces the magma to the surface. Here it breaks through weak or thin spots in the crust, creating subduction volcanoes.

Spreading ridges/mid-ocean ridges

A spreading ridge is a region where two tectonic plates move apart. Molten magma then rises up into the opening, creating new crust. Also known as mid-ocean ridges, **submarine** volcanoes are found here.

Converging plates

Unlike subduction, sometimes when plates collide they push each other upwards creating huge mountain ranges. These mountains are often volcanic.

There are seven major plates and many smaller ones. The plates move about 5 cm every year.

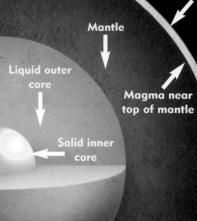

Crust

Mantle

Liquid outer core

Magma near top of mantle

Solid inner core

Spreading ridges/mid-ocean ridges
As the plates move apart the rising magma usually sticks to the side of the plates and solidifies. Sometimes the magma will reach the surface and create volcanoes.

Subduction volcanoes
The descending plate melts to form magma. This magma can then rise to the surface and create volcanoes.

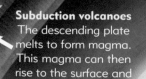

Converging plates
When two plates meet head-on sometimes the rock is too light so instead of subduction occurring the plates buckle and are pushed upwards. The Himalayas were created this way millions of years ago when the Indian and Eurasian plates met.

Eruption! Why Do Volcanoes Erupt?

As magma rises, gases expand and water becomes steam. This creates huge pressure. When the pressure becomes too great, a volcano erupts. Eruptions can range from gentle oozing, to violent explosions.

Over time, magma collects in the magma chamber, deep underneath a volcano. Because magma is lighter than the surrounding rock it rises towards the surface, just as a cork floats in water. While rising through the **crater pipe** and **vents**, bubbles of gas begin to form.

Viscosity

Eruptions can be a trickle of lava or an enormous explosion. This depends on the **viscosity** of the magma – how sticky it is – and its gas content. When magma is highly viscous, with lots of gas, the eruption will be violent. This is because gas finds it more difficult to escape from sticky magma. As the gas increases, it exerts great pressure. The pressure finally causes the magma to erupt violently through the vent. Once magma hits the surface it is called lava.

When huge amounts of ash and gas explode out of the volcano, terrifying and deadly **pyroclastic flows** can result. These destructive flows of boiling gas and ash tumble at great speed down the slopes destroying everything in their paths.

Eruptions are less intense if the magma is less viscous, because the gas escapes more easily.

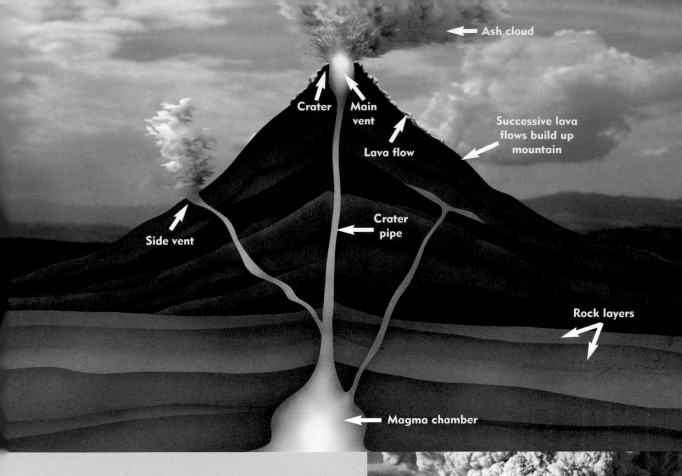

Ash cloud

Crater

Main vent

Successive lava flows build up mountain

Lava flow

Side vent

Crater pipe

Rock layers

Magma chamber

Gas-rich magma is much more explosive than magma that contains less gas.

GO FACT!

DID YOU KNOW?

When vents are blocked by material from previous eruptions, huge pressure builds up inside the volcano. This can lead to explosive eruptions, such as the eruption of Mount St. Helens in 1980 – 275 million tonnes of material was ejected from the volcano.

The Aftermath of Eruptions

The ash, poisonous gases and mud slides that follow an eruption can have the greatest impact on people and the landscape.

Ash

Volcanic ash is deadly. It is hard and abrasive, like finely crushed glass. After blasting into the air, it forms an **eruption plume**, which settles over huge areas, suffocating people and animals.

Gas

Gases spewed out from volcanic eruptions, such as carbon dioxide and sulphur dioxide, are even more deadly. As carbon dioxide is heavier than air, it collects in low-lying areas and creates poisonous environments. Sulphur dioxide causes acid rain and air pollution.

Lahars

Devastating mudflows, known as **lahars**, are caused by ash, soil and rock combining on volcanic slopes. Lahars also occur when snow melts because of the heat of an eruption. The snow mixes with soil and fallen ash, ripping houses and trees from the ground, carrying them downstream. In 1985 an eruption of the Nevado del Ruiz volcano in Colombia led to lahars that buried the town of Armero, killing 23 000 people.

In 1995 a relentless rain of ash virtually buried the city of New Plymouth on the Caribbean island of Montserrat. Once a thriving capital it is now a ghost town, covered in more than a metre of volcanic ash.

A small amount of ash fall can fertilise soils, but too much will destroy vegetation.

GO FACT!

DID YOU KNOW?

When Mount Pinatubo in the Philippines erupted in 1991, it blocked out sunlight for days. Over 800 people were killed.

You can make a volcano. Be careful – erupting volcanoes are messy and yours will be no different.

What you need:
- empty plastic detergent or small drink bottle
- play dough
- a cup of white vinegar
- red food colouring and red glitter
- half a cup of water
- one heaped tablespoon of bicarbonate of soda

1 Pour vinegar into the bottle so the bottle is one third full. Add some red food colouring and glitter.

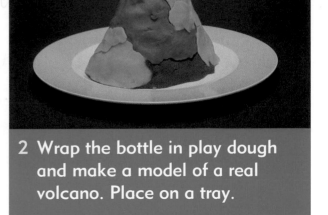

2 Wrap the bottle in play dough and make a model of a real volcano. Place on a tray.

3 Mix the water and bicarbonate of soda together in a separate container.

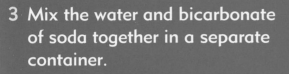

4 Pour this mixture into the bottle and watch your volcano erupt. What sort of volcanic eruption does it look like?

Making a pyroclastic flow:

Pyroclastic flows are clouds of boiling hot gas and ash that sweep down the sides of a volcano at speeds of up to 100–150 kilometres per hour (60–95 miles per hour) and reach temperatures of 800 °C.

Here's how to make a pyroclastic flow for your volcano. Repeat all the steps but this time add a few drops of washing up liquid to the vinegar in step 4. The frothy liquid that bubbles out of the bottle and flows down the side is similar to a pyroclastic flow.

13

Volcanoes of the World

Mount St Helens

Mount Kilauea

Mount Pinatubo

Krakatoa

Pacific Ocean

About three quarters of the world's volcanoes are found in the 'Ring of Fire' which follows the edge of the Pacific Ocean. Africa, Europe and even icy Antarctica are also home to erupting volcanoes.

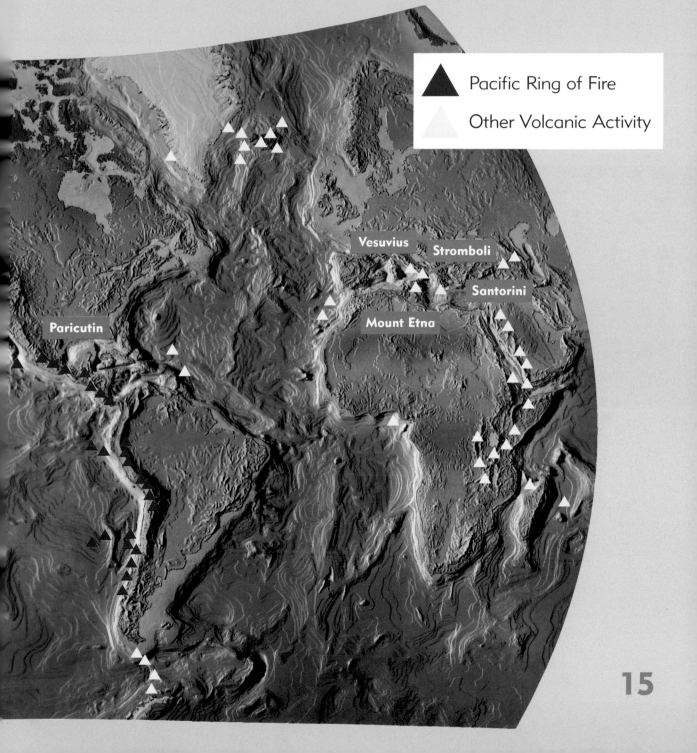

Pacific Ring of Fire

Other Volcanic Activity

Vesuvius

Stromboli

Santorini

Mount Etna

Paricutin

Types of Volcano

The three main types of volcano are composite, shield and cinder cone volcanoes. Other volcanoes form over hot spots in the Earth's mantle.

Composite volcanoes erupt rarely, with gaps of hundreds of years between eruptions.

Composite volcanoes

Also known as stratovolcanoes, composite volcanoes are formed by layers of lava and rock fragments. The lava is viscous, which clogs up the crater pipe, trapping gas. This increased pressure results in destructive eruptions, known as *Plinian eruptions*.

Shield volcanoes

Occurring at **hot spots**, these are the largest volcanoes. As they are formed by runny lava, their slopes are gentle, spreading over large areas. Erupting every few years, they create **lava flows** and **fire fountains**. Hawaiian volcanoes are shield volcanoes. Their eruptions are called *Hawaiian eruptions*.

More than 4 km (2.5 miles) above sea level, Mauna Loa, a shield volcano, is the largest volcano in the world. It covers half the island of Hawaii.

Cinder cones can reach 250 metres in height and 500 metres in diameter. They usually occur in groups, often near composite or shield volcanoes.

Cinder cone volcanoes

These volcanoes have steep slopes and very wide **summit craters**. Their eruptions do not produce much lava. Instead lava fragments, called cinders, and **tephra** are ejected into the air. These eruptions are known as *Strombolian eruptions*.

Hot spot volcanoes

Hot spots are very hot regions in Earth's mantle. Hot spots are permanent **reservoirs** of magma that break through the tectonic plates as they move overhead, forming chains of volcanoes. The Hawaiian and Galapagos Islands formed when plates moved over hot spots.

GO FACT!

DID YOU KNOW?

The Galapagos Islands formed when plates moved over hot spots.

Types of Eruption

Volcanoes behave in different ways. The type of eruption forms the shape of the volcano. This also affects the surrounding landscape and its people.

Plinian eruptions

Plinian eruptions are often spectacular and dangerous. Gas-rich magma explodes, sending gas, ash and cinders up to 45 kilometres (28 miles) skywards in an eruption plume. They can create pyroclastic flows covering everything in their path. Ash drifts for thousands of kilometres and the initial explosion can trigger landslides, mudflows and floods.

Hawaiian eruptions

Named after the Hawaiian Islands where many of these volcano types are found, Hawaiian volcanoes are low-pressure volcanoes. The lava that emerges is thick and slow flowing. Though sluggish they are steady – Mount Kilauea has been erupting since 1983, making it one of the world's most active volcanoes.

Strombolian eruptions

These eruptions are named after the volcanic island of Stromboli in the Mediterranean Sea. Small amounts of thick lava, steam and gas are ejected into the air frequently, sometimes reaching up to 1000 metres into the atmosphere. Stromboli itself erupts every 15–30 minutes, shooting lava blocks and gases.

Mount Kilauea has been erupting since 1983, making it the longest continuous eruption of the 20th century.

Ancient Greek sailors used the glow from Stromboli's crater to navigate their ships.

Plinian eruptions normally erupt from composite volcanoes.

GO FACT!

DID YOU KNOW?

The Mount Vesuvius eruption of 79 AD was a Plinian eruption. It buried Pompeii and killed more than 2000 people. Pompeii remained buried for over 1500 years.

Mount St. Helens

In 1980, on the morning of May 18th, Mount St. Helens in Washington State, USA, erupted. The explosive eruption lasted for nine hours and resulted in the deaths of 57 people. It caused immense damage to the surrounding wildlife and landscape.

A mountain stirs

Mount St. Helens had been quiet for over a century when in March 1980, small earth tremors and eruptions of gas and rock began. A bulge appeared on its northern side, which grew 90 metres high by mid-May. There were frequent earth tremors. Authorities kept sightseers away.

A mountain explodes

On the 18th, geologists circling the summit in a light aircraft saw the north face 'ripple and churn' before it suddenly collapsed. An enormous explosion followed blasting out millions of tonnes of rock and ash. A plume shot 20 km (12 miles) skywards.

The collapse triggered a landslide of 8000 million tonnes of rock and ice. It reached speeds of 290 km/h (190 mph).

The initial blast travelled at 1200 km/h (745 mph), devastated 52 000 hectares of land and flattened everything 12 km (7.5 miles) northwards. Lightning flashed in the clouds of ash, and burning embers started over 300 forest fires during the nine-hour eruption.

In geological terms, the Mount St. Helens eruption was mild!

The blast was heard 320 km (200 miles) away and the ash cloud ended up travelling 1500 km (932 miles) across the USA.

DID YOU KNOW?
The number of trees blown down by the **lateral blast** of the eruption could have built 300 000 homes.

Before

After

The force of the explosion that blew away much of the summit of Mount St. Helens was equal to that of a 10-megaton hydrogen bomb — 500 times the power of the atom bomb dropped on Hiroshima in the dying days of World War II.

Volcanic Landscapes

Areas around volcanoes are called geothermal regions. Magma near the Earth's surface heats the surrounding rocks. The rocks then heat the ground water to high temperatures.

Hot springs

Hot springs are often found in geothermal regions. Also known as thermal springs, they form when rising magma warms the surrounding rock and **ground water**. The water becomes extremely hot and forces its way to the surface, escaping as a hot spring.

Geysers

Geysers are hot springs erupting from vents in the ground. They occur when ground water becomes trapped in an underground cavity. Heat rising from a magma chamber warms the trapped water. The water boils due to the intense heat, and turns into steam. The steam builds up inside the cavity which increases the pressure. Finally, the pressure is so strong it forces the water and steam upwards and out through the vent, high into the air.

Mud pools

Mud pools are created when hot water and steam rise up through soft soil and ash, rather than hard rock. The liquid mixes with the soil to form bubbling pools of hot mud.

Some geysers erupt on a regular basis. A geyser called 'Old Faithful' in Yellowstone National Park, USA, erupts every hour or so.

The water in hot springs may be pure and clear, but it often contains minerals from the rocks it passed through on its way to the surface.

GO FACT!

DID YOU KNOW?

The word 'geyser' comes from the Icelandic region and means 'to rush forth' or 'to gush'.

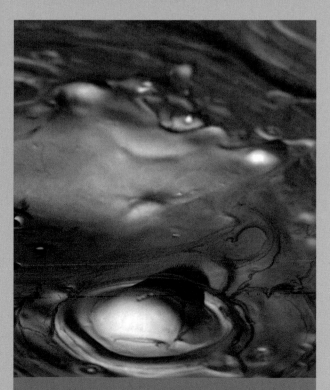

Some people believe that volcanic mud has healing powers.

23

Living with Volcanoes

All around the world people and volcanoes exist side by side. Though volcanoes pose a threat, living near volcanoes can also provide advantages.

Volcanic soils

Volcanic soils are very fertile, making them ideal for growing crops. Indonesian farmers grow rice near active volcanoes. However, thick lava flows are disastrous. It takes months for lava to cool, and then years for soil to form.

Ancient eruption, modern money maker

In Italy, previous eruptions provide daily benefits. The Roman city Pompeii, buried when Mount Vesuvius erupted in 79 AD, now attracts thousands of visitors. Spending by these tourists helps the local economy.

However, Mount Vesuvius, is still active. Millions could be affected by a new eruption. Volcanic activity has brought benefits to southern Italy, but eruptions are a constant threat.

Energy and minerals

Ground water, heated by magma, is used to make geothermal energy. Steam from high-temperature ground water creates electrical power. Ground water with a lower temperature heats homes and also provides bathing water. Geothermal energy is the second-largest source of energy in Iceland.

Minerals are also useful by-products of volcanic activity. Many minerals, such as gold, silver and copper are mined from the magma of extinct volcanoes after it has cooled and hardened.

Archaeological digs at Pompeii have provided us with much knowledge about the daily lives of ancient Romans.

The energy from the geothermal region in Svartsengi, Iceland, is used to produce electricity.

Mount Etna in Italy is Europe's highest active volcano.

GO FACT!

DID YOU KNOW?

In 1992 an eruption of Mount Etna threatened to bury the village of Zafferana under a river of lava. They used a combination of explosives, earth barriers and large concrete blocks to divert the lava flow. Though the village was saved, homes and buildings on its outskirts were destroyed.

Working with Volcanoes

Volcanologists are scientists who study volcanoes. They try to find out how volcanoes form and predict when they might erupt.

Tuesday, 4:30 a.m.

Pasto, Colombia: Up early, as low cloud will mean the summit of the Galeras volcano is covered by mid-morning. Am taking two geology students with me today so need to give them a 'health and safety' talk once we're on the summit. Because of the students I'll stick to the outer rim and just take a few **core samples** and some readings with the **seismograph**.

9 a.m.

Cold on the summit – strange how the air temperature is so cool but the rocks I'm standing on would burn through the soles of a normal pair of boots. Mist and steam are swirling everywhere and the smell of sulphur is stronger than last week. We are all dressed in our protective gear so it's time to get to work.

11 a.m.

Back at the lower base camp. Today's readings were OK – three lava samples and some ground monitoring. Have emailed the seismo readings to the lab in Bogotá and will send lava with the courier tomorrow. The seismograph indicated many small tremors.

Despite the heat from the lava the air temperature is quite cool, as can be seen by my heavy jacket.

Capturing the moment. Set-up the camera to take self-portrait, with students.

Seismographs measure tremors in the Earth, which help scientists to predict when a volcano might erupt.

Scientists cannot prevent volcanoes from erupting. They try to predict when an eruption will occur, and with what force, so they can try to save lives.

Timeline

Santorini, Mediterranean
Huge eruption destroyed 80 square kilometres (31 square miles) of the island. Some believe this was the 'lost city of Atlantis'.

Vesuvius, Italy
The ash from the eruption buried the Roman towns of Pompeii, Herculaneum and Stabiae for over 1500 years.

1620 BC

79 AD

Surtsey, Iceland
A new island grew as a result of undersea volcanic activity. After 10 days it was 900 metres long and 650 metres wide. Three years later plants, insects and birds had colonised the island.

Paricutin, Mexico
A volcano sprung up in a cornfield overnight. It grew 168 metres in a week. After nine years of activity it was 412 metres high.

1963

1943

Heimay, Iceland
One third of the town was swallowed by a lava flow up to six metres deep. It added 2.5 square kilometres (0.9 square miles) of land to the island.

Mount St. Helens, USA
Explosion caused massive damage to the beautiful mountain region of Washington State, leaving 600 square kilometres (232 square miles) as barren wasteland.

1973

1980

Skaftar, Iceland
Lava covered 580 square kilometres (224 square miles) of land. Dust settled over Europe, Africa and Asia leading to climate changes and famines. Largest lava flow in recorded history.

Tambora, Indonesia
Most powerful eruption in recorded history. Eighty times the power of Mount St. Helens. The following Northern Hemisphere summer was called the 'year without a summer'.

1783

1815

Mount Pelee, Martinique, Caribbean
A huge pyroclastic flow claimed 30 000 lives. There were two survivors – a shoemaker living on the edge of town and a prisoner whose underground cell protected him.

Krakatoa, Indonesia
Two-thirds of uninhabited island blown away by huge explosions. Caused a tsunami which destroyed 165 villages. A new island, Anak Krakatoa (Child of Krakatoa), was created.

1902

1883

Pinatubo, Philippines
The most violent eruption of the 20th century. After remaining dormant for 400 years the eruption blotted out daylight in the region for days, and blew 200 metres of the mountain top away.

Nevado del Ruiz, Colombia
Had not erupted for nearly 150 years. Eruption caused mud slides which buried four towns in the region, killing about 23 000 people.

1981

1985

Types of Volcanoes and Eruptions

Type of Volcano	Type of Eruption	Volcanoes of the World
Composite	Plinian	Agua, Guatemala Hekla, Iceland Irazú Volcano, Costa Rica Klyuchevskaya, Russia Mount Cotopaxi, Ecuador Mount Fuji, Japan Mount Mayon, Luzon Mount Pinatubo, Philippines Mount St. Helens, Washington, USA Nevado del Ruiz, Colombia
Cinder Cone	Strombolian	Amboy, California, USA Cerro Negro, Nicaragua Heimay, Iceland Paricutin, Mexico Red Cones, California, USA Sunset Crater, Arizona, USA Surtsey, Iceland
Shield	Hawaiian	Alcedo, Galápagos Islands Fernandina, Galápagos Islands Mauna Kea, Hawaii Mauna Loa, Hawaii Mount Kilauea, Hawaii
Caldera	Plinian	Krakatoa, Indonesia Santorini, Greece

Some volcanoes display more than one type of eruption.

Type of Volcano	Type of Eruption	Volcanoes of the World
Composite	Plinian/Strombolian Hawaiian/Plinian Hawaiian/Plinian/Strombolian Hawaiian/Plinian/Strombolian Hawaiian/Plinian/Strombolian	Mount Etna, Italy Mount Pelée, Caribbean Mount Vesuvius, Italy Stromboli, Italy Tambora, Indonesia

Glossary

caldera a large crater formed when a volcano collapses in on itself

core samples samples of lava taken from within a volcano that tells how old the volcano is and how it formed

crater pipe a tube connecting a magma chamber to the surface

eruption plume a stream of gas, ash and steam forced skyward by an eruption

fire fountains fountains of bright, orange lava shooting high into the air

ground water water just below the surface of the ground

hot spots areas underneath the Earth's crust where the rocks are hotter than elsewhere

lahars Indonesian word for fast-moving flow of rock debris and water that begins on a volcano slope; volcanic mudflows

lateral blast horizontal clouds of gases and extremely hot, rock particles that explode outwards at very high speeds from a volcano

lava flows lava which flows down the side of a volcano after it overflows the rim of a crater or vent

magma chamber hollow space underground where magma collects

mantle layer below Earth's crust that is partly molten

pyroclastic flows flows of boiling hot gas, mixed with ash and cinders, that can sweep down volcanic slopes at speeds of over 100 km/h (62 mph), reaching temperatures between 100 and 800 degrees Celsius

reservoirs cavities that hold liquid

seismograph an instrument that measures vibrations within the Earth's surface

submarine under the surface of the sea

summit craters mouths of volcanoes where the lava exits

tephra volcanic rock, lava and ash that are blasted into the air from a crater or volcanic vent and deposited close to the volcano

tsunamis large waves caused by an undersea earthquake

vents openings in the Earth's surface that allows molten rock and gases to escape

viscosity stickiness; thickness; ability to resist flow

# Index